Childrens Aliens and Monsters Coloring Book

My Crazy Monsters Coloring Fun

Grace Sure

Copyright

All rights reserved. No part of this book may be reproduced or transferred in any form or by any means without the written permission of the publisher and author. This publication is Copyright 2015 by World Ideas Ltd / BLEP Publishing.

All rights reserved.
ISBN:
978-1-910085-56-1

What's Inside?

My Crazy Monsters Coloring Fun – One of the year's best coloring books for young children.

Monsters and aliens Coloring Book – Each wonderful image is drawn specially for children to enjoy. They'll have hours of fun coloring in these creative monster designs (and don't forget by buying THIS book you can print out copies of all images inside as many times as you wish – details inside)

A coloring book that never runs out...

Buy the book today and I'll give you a link where you can print out as many copies of all the images as you want (perfect for kids and great for sharing with their friends). Plus when they want to recolor any picture, you can simply print it out and let them show off their coloring skills in new ways.

Let their artistic expression run free and enjoy all the benefits it brings. It's widely reported that it helps improve hand to eye coordination and helps improve muscles in hands, wrists and fingers.

Plus it helps improve patience and concentration (a highly valuable skill) which can help them develop further and progress faster.

You may notice they also start to plan ahead (a great life skill) the colors they'll use and the order they're going to complete it in.

Since there is no right or wrong way to color, they'll feel a great sense of accomplishment coloring in.

Coloring provides relaxed, peaceful calm time away from TV's, computers and other electronic devices. Let them enjoy this wonderful past-time without pressure.

Extra Bonus

You'll also receive a wonderful free bonus of 10 extra images from our other childrens coloring books for them to enjoy.

Start Coloring Today...

Enjoy Coloring?

Over the next few pages please find images from some of our other childrens coloring books.

If you like them please just search for them by book title (listed under each image) or by the ISBN online so you can enjoy the complete coloring book.

All Our Childrens Coloring Books

ABC

Alphabet ABC Coloring Book - My First ABC and 123 Numbers Coloring Book
ISBN: 978-1-910085-32-5

Christmas

Christmas Coloring Book for Children - Santa's Magical Christmas Coloring Book for Children
ISBN: 978-1-910085-97-4

Christmas Coloring Book for Kids - Rudolph and Santa's Christmas Coloring Book for Kids
ISBN: 978-1-910085-96-7

Cute

Cute Animal Coloring Book for Kids - My Adorable, Cuddly and Very Cute Coloring Book
ISBN: 978-1-910085-68-4

Cute Coloring Book for Children - My Incredibly Cute Animal Coloring Book
ISBN: 978-1-910085-67-7

Dinosaurs

Dinosaur Coloring Book To Make You Roar!
ISBN: 978-1-910085-60-8

Halloween

Kids Halloween Coloring Book - Childrens Creative Halloween Coloring Books
ISBN: 978-1-910085-93-6

Halloween Coloring Book - Ghosts, Witches, Monsters, Haunted Houses and More... - Art Halloween Books for Children
ISBN: 978-1-910085-92-9

Monsters and Aliens

Childrens Aliens and Monsters Coloring Book - My Crazy Monsters Coloring Fun
ISBN: 978-1-910085-56-1

Monster and Aliens Coloring Book for Kids - Monsters, Aliens and More Monsters Coloring
ISBN: 978-1-910085-54-7

Robots

Robot Coloring Book - My Monster Robot Coloring Fun For Kids
ISBN: 978-1-910085-48-6

Coloring Robots - My Robot Machines Fun Coloring For Children
ISBN: 978-1-910085-46-2

Summer Holidays

Kids Summer Holiday Fun Coloring Book - Perfect for Coloring on Childrens Car, Plane and Train Journeys
ISBN: 978-1-910085-91-2

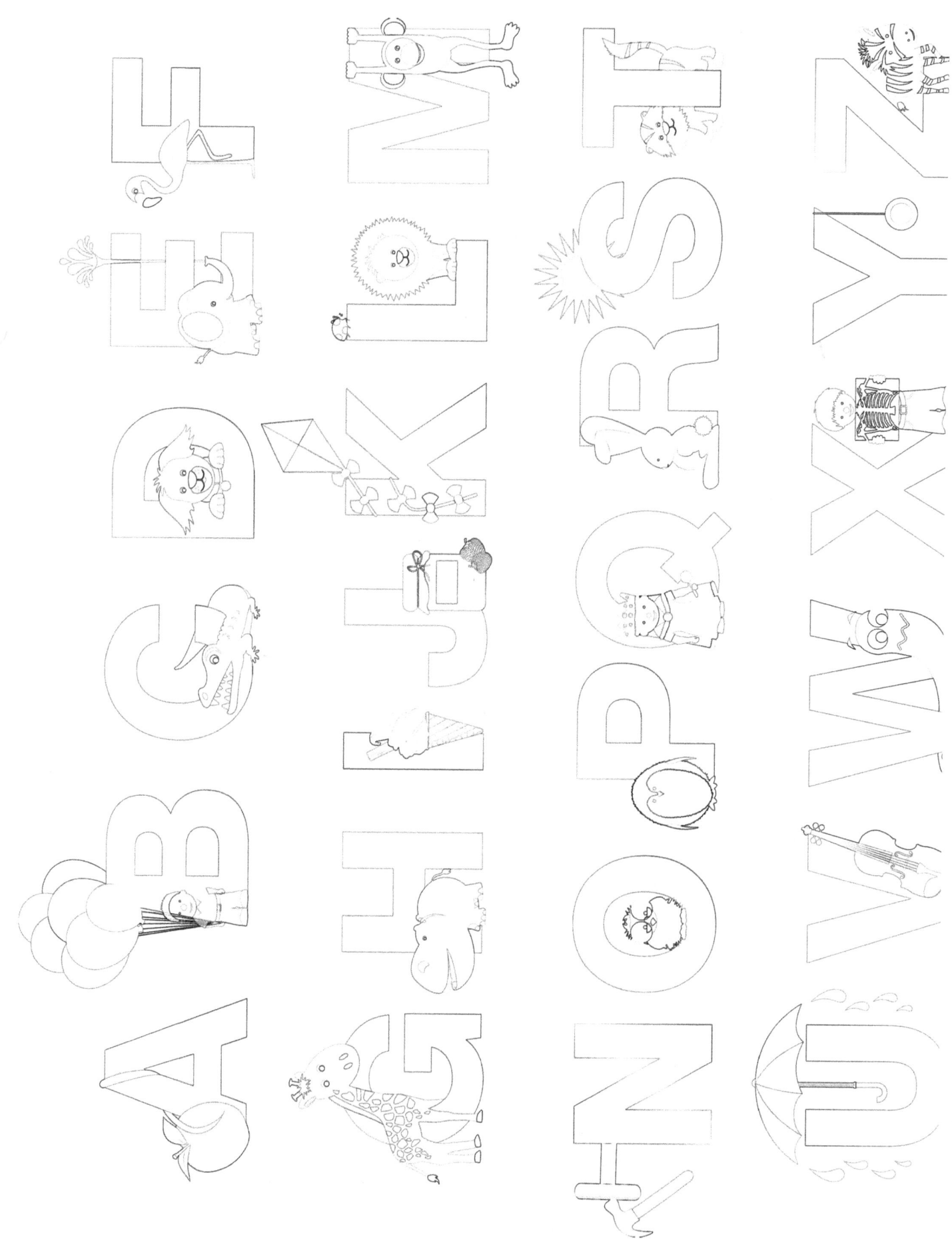

FROM: Alphabet ABC Coloring Book - My First ABC and 123 Numbers Coloring Book - ISBN: 978-1-910085-32-5

FROM: Christmas Coloring Book for Children - Santa's Magical Christmas Coloring Book for Children - ISBN: 978-1-910085-97-4

From: Christmas Coloring Book for Kids - Rudolph and Santa's Christmas Coloring Book for Kids - ISBN: 978-1-910085-96-7

From: Cute Animal Coloring Book for Kids - My Adorable, Cuddly and Very Cute Coloring Book - ISBN: 978-1-910085-68-4

From: Cute Coloring Book for Children - My Incredibly Cute Animal Coloring Book - ISBN: 978-1-910085-67-7

From: Kids Halloween Coloring Book - Childrens Creative Halloween Coloring Books - ISBN: 978-1-910085-93-6

From: Halloween Coloring Book - Ghosts, Witches, Monsters, Haunted Houses and More... - Art Halloween Books for Children ISBN: 978-1-910085-92-9

From: Monster and Aliens Coloring Book for Kids - Monsters, Aliens and More Monsters Coloring - ISBN: 978-1-910085-54-7

From: Robot Coloring Book - My Monster Robot Coloring Fun For Kids
ISBN: 978-1-910085-48-6

From: Coloring Robots - My Robot Machines Fun Coloring For Children
ISBN: 978-1-910085-46-2

From: Kids Summer Holiday Fun Coloring Book - Perfect for Coloring on Childrens Car, Plane and Train Journeys - ISBN: 978-1-910085-91-2

All Our Adult Coloring Books
Coloring Books Designed for Artists, Adults, Teens and Older Children

Beautiful Birds

Bird Coloring Book Including Owls for Adults - Bird Paradise - My Beautiful Coloring Book
ISBN: 978-1-910085-74-5

Owls & Other Birds Coloring Book for Grown Ups: - On The Wings Of A Dove Coloring
ISBN: 978-1-910085-73-8

Cuddly Cats

Cat Coloring Book For Adults - My Captivating Creative Cat Designs and Patterns Artists Favorite Coloring Books
ISBN: 978-1-910085-30-1

Cats Coloring Book Creative Designs - Cute Little Cats Needing My Artistic Care
ISBN: 978-1-910085-29-5

Christmas Magic

Christmas Coloring Book for Adults - Fantastically Festive Patterns and Designs for Christmas Sparkle
ISBN: 978-1-910085-72-1

Christmas Coloring Book for Grownups - Santa and Rudolphs Classic Christmas Delights
ISBN: 978-1-910085-71-4

City Style

City Coloring Book for Adults - Fantastic Cities, Splendid Creative Designs
ISBN: 978-1-910085-70-7

City Coloring Book - My Secret City Creative Coloring Book for Adults and Older Children
ISBN: 978-1-910085-69-1

Doodling Doddles

Doodle Coloring Book to Color My Stress Away - Adult Art Doodle Coloring Book Enjoy the Creative Invasion!
ISBN: 978-1-910085-95-0

Doodle Coloring Books: - Relaxing Art Doodle Designs and Patterns
ISBN: 978-1-910085-94-3

Flower Delights

Flower Coloring Book for Adults - Beautiful Creative Floral Flower Designs and Patterns
ISBN: 978-1-910085-66-0

Nature Garden Flowers Coloring Book for Adults - Garden Flowers in Full Bloom in My Creative Designs
ISBN: 978-1-910085-65-3

Adult Coloring Book of Flowers - Bouquets, Roses, Garden Flowers a Creative Flower Coloring Masterpiece
ISBN: 978-1-910085-64-6

Geometric Magic

Geometric Coloring Book for Adults - Intricate Geometric Coloring Designs for Adults – Creative Color Your Imagination
ISBN: 978-1-910085-99-8

Geometric Coloring Book for Adults - Geometric Coloring – Book of Surprising Wonders
ISBN: 978-1-910085-98-1

Hippie Life

Hippie Coloring Book - Peace, Love and Hippies Coloring
ISBN: 978-1-910085-63-9

Coloring Book for Hippies - Relieve My Magical Hippie 70's and Feel the Love
ISBN: 978-1-910085-62-2

Love In My Heart

Peace and Love Coloring Book - My Beautiful Valentine Love Coloring Book with Gorgeous Designs
ISBN: 978-1-910085-61-5

Love Coloring Book for Adults - Creative Love of My Heart
ISBN: 978-1-910085-58-5

Mystic Mandalas

Mandala Coloring Book for Meditation – Effective Relaxation and Anti-Stress Mandalas
ISBN: 978-1-910085-90-5

Mandala Coloring Books for Adults - Coloring Creative Mystical Mandala Designs and Patterns for Relaxation and Meditation
ISBN: 978-1-910085-89-9

Mandala Artists Coloring Book - Beautiful Magical Mandalas to Color Today
ISBN: 978-1-910085-88-2

Mosaic Pieces

Mosaic Coloring Books for Adults - My Magical Mosaic Coloring Masterpieces
ISBN: 978-1-910085-87-5

Mosaic Coloring Fun Book - Creative Fun Mosaic Patterns and Designs
ISBN: 978-1-910085-86-8

Music Masters

Music Coloring Book for Adults - Color My Music, Fill My Passion
ISBN: 978-1-910085-52-3

Music Coloring Book - Love Music, Love Color
ISBN: 978-1-910085-50-9

Paisley Patterns

Paisley Coloring Book for Adults - Creative Coloring Paisley Patterns and Designs for Perfect Relaxation
ISBN: 978-1-910085-85-1

Paisley Coloring Book - Stunning Mystical Paisley Designs and Patterns
ISBN: 978-1-910085-84-4

Relaxing Patterns

Pattern Coloring Book - Detailed, Beautiful and Wonderfully Creative Coloring Patterns
ISBN: 978-1-910085-83-7

Adult Pattern Coloring Book - Modern, Detailed Artistic Pattern Adult Coloring Book for Relaxation
ISBN: 978-1-910085-82-0

Coloring Patterns - Unique Creative Pattern Masterpieces Designed for Artists
ISBN: 978-1-910085-81-3

Pattern Coloring Book For Adults - Color Me Patterns, Calm Relaxation Coloring Therapy
ISBN: 978-1-910085-80-6

Coloring Pattern Book - Imagination On Paper Coloring Patterns
ISBN: 978-1-910085-79-0

Spring / Easter Surprise

Headers: Easter & Spring Coloring Book - Creative Designs and Patterns for Adults and Older Children
ISBN: 978-1-910085-78-3

Spring and Easter Coloring Book - Hop Into Easter
ISBN: 978-1-910085-77-6

Sugarskull – Day of the Dead!

Sugar Skull Adult Coloring Book - Day Of The Dead Mexican Creative Sugar Skull Designs
ISBN: 978-1-910085-76-9

Sugar Skull: Dia De Los Muertos / Day Of The Dead - Coloring Book for Grown Ups
ISBN: 978-1-910085-75-2

Stained Glass Wonders

Stained Glass Wonders Coloring Book
ISBN: 978-1-910085-59-2

Tattoo Art

Tattoo Coloring Book: - My Creative Body Art Tattoo Designs
ISBN: 978-1-910085-44-8

Tattoo Coloring Book for Adults - Coloring Tattoos My Fantastic Body Art
ISBN: 978-1-910085-42-4

Wildlife Wonders

Wildlife Coloring Book - Forest Elephants, Giraffes, African Big Cats and More, Natures Wildlife Coloring Art
ISBN: 978-1-910085-36-3

Wildlife Coloring Book for Adults - Explore Wildlife in Natures Magnificent Animal Kingdom
ISBN: 978-1-910085-34-9

About Me

I have loved drawing from a very young age and now it is my pleasure to share with you a collection of my favorite images. I've spent months putting these together for you, I really hope you enjoy them. I have tried to include something for everyone, some with lots of detail others less for when you want to complete an image within a shorter time and with a wide range of images.

The benefits of coloring have been widely reported. The Huffington Post reported "The practice generates wellness, quietness and also stimulates brain" they go on to say "In simplest terms, coloring has a de-stressing effect because when we focus on a particular activity, we focus on it and not on our worries. But it also "brings out our imagination and takes us back to our childhood, a period in which we most certainly had a lot less stress."

I hope you've enjoyed coloring these designs – Please can you help me?

Hopefully you've enjoyed coloring some or all of these images. Please, please, please can you take the time to share your thoughts and post a review on whatever site you purchased it from. It will be greatly appreciated and really help me – thank you.

Don't Forget

If you want to recolor any of these designs again you can and get more free images please just visit http://coloringfans.com/aliens

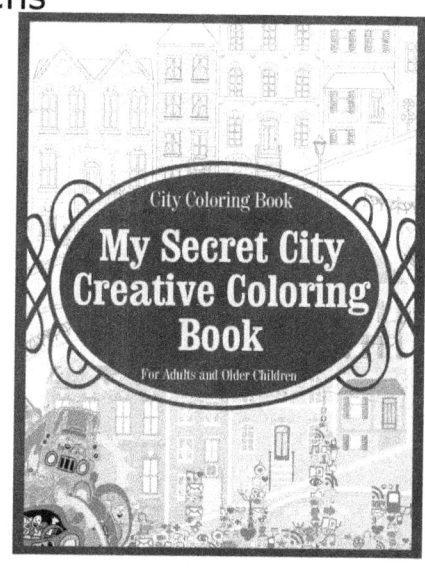

MORE FREE COLORING IMAGES...

Would you like to color some or all of these images again? Perhaps in different colors or styles. Now you can print out as many copies as you like. I'll send you every design in this book free.

Please just visit
http://coloringfans.com/aliens
so I can send you all the designs today.

Thank you so much for purchasing this book. I hope you have many happy hours coloring in all the wonderful images.

As an extra 'thank you' I would be delighted if you join our free club. I'll email you all the designs as a pdf document so you can just print them off at home as many times as you like - you can even print them for your friends, please just mention us. Just don't upload them on-line, publish them, sell them, or claim they are yours!

Plus I'll send you advance designs of our new coloring books (before they are released) for you to enjoy free.

If you'd like to 'show off' your skills I'm also putting together a gallery of your achievements. Details included when you join free.

http://coloringfans.com/aliens

Please visit today

Thank you

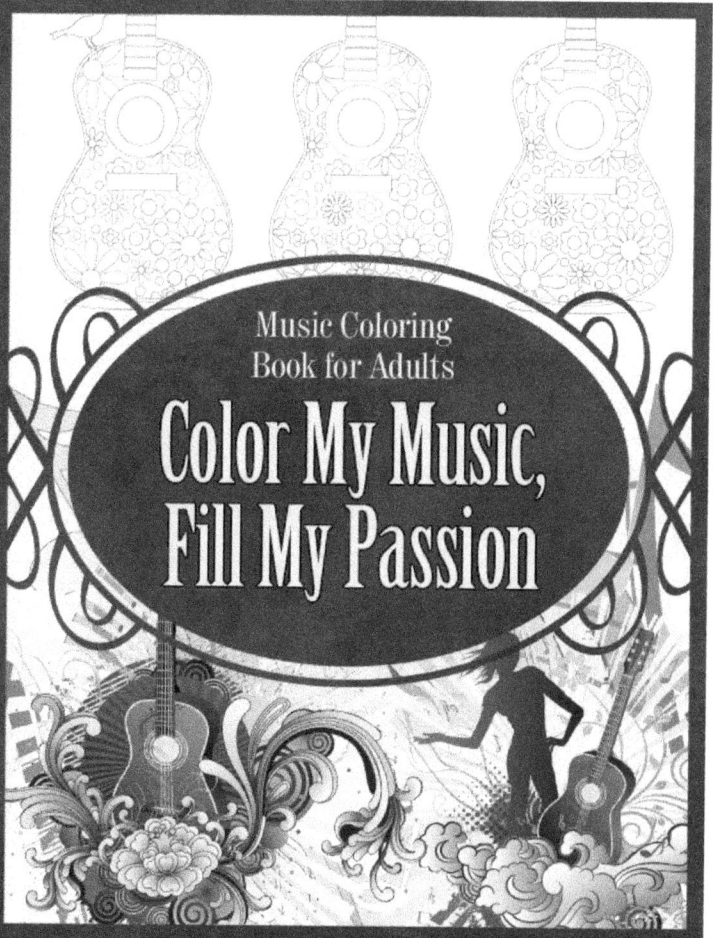

www.ingramcontent.com/pod-product-compliance
Lightning Source LLC
Chambersburg PA
CBHW080523030426
42337CB00023B/4604